STRENGTH FOR YOUR FUTURE

STRENGTH FOR YOUR FUTURE

Conservative Principles That Can
SECURE YOUR SUCCESS

WILLIAM J. BENNETT
AND JOHN T. E. CRIBB

Tyndale House Publishers, Inc.
Carol Stream, Illinois

Visit Tyndale online at www.tyndale.com.

TYNDALE, Tyndale's quill logo, and *LeatherLike* are registered trademarks of Tyndale House Publishers, Inc.

Strength for Your Future: Conservative Principles That Can Secure Your Success

Designed by Dean H. Renninger

All Scripture quotations, unless otherwise indicated, are taken from the Holy Bible, *New International Version*,® *NIV*.® Copyright © 1973, 1978, 1984, 2011 by Biblica, Inc.® Used by permission. All rights reserved worldwide.

Scripture quotations marked KJV are taken from the *Holy Bible*, King James Version.

Library of Congress Cataloging-in-Publication Data
Names: Bennett, William J. (William John), date, author.
Title: Strength for your future : principles that can secure your success /
    William J. Bennett and John T. E. Cribb.
Description: Carol Stream, IL : Tyndale House Publishers, Inc., 2016. |
    Includes bibliographical references.
Identifiers: LCCN 2015039472 | ISBN 9781496405951 (leatherlike)
Subjects: LCSH: Conservatism—United States. | Conduct of life. | Social
    values—United States. | United States—Moral conditions.
Classification: LCC JC573.2.U6 B463 2016 | DDC 320.520973—dc23 LC record available
at http://lccn.loc.gov/2015039472

Printed in China

22   21   20   19   18   17   16
7   6   5   4   3   2   1

CONTENTS

A WORD OF ADVICE
TO YOUNG AMERICANS

YOU HAVE REACHED A TIME IN LIFE when you'll begin to ask yourself some important questions: *What am I going to do with myself? How am I going to make a living? How will I be successful? What do I find fulfilling? How do I live a good life?*

You're not going to figure out the answers all at once. It will take a while. Some of the questions may change over time. It's a long process that's a big part of adulthood.

There are lots of places you can look for advice. Start with adults you know and trust—your parents, most of all. Grandparents. Teachers. Coaches. Clergy. Members of your house of worship. They have traveled the road you are on now, and they can help you along your way.

Great books—starting with the Bible—are loaded with clues about how to live a successful life and how

1

to avoid trouble. The classics you may have met in high school (like *Pride and Prejudice* or *Macbeth*) are full of insights. They're definitely worth second and third looks. Biographies of great lives like Abraham Lincoln and Mother Teresa will help guide you. Some of those bestselling advice books on the shelves at the library or bookstore can be useful too.

There is one source of guidance that's often overlooked—your country. The United States is one of the greatest success stories in history. It didn't get that way by accident.

At the core of this nation are some ideas and principles that have made it great, principles that are worth studying and knowing for many reasons. One reason is that, just as those principles have made our country good and successful, they can help each of us live good, successful lives.

So here's a word of advice about success: study, know, and love America and its principles. The United States is an unparalleled model of achievement. Any such model is worth studying. It's worth asking, *How in the world has it achieved so much? What has it done right? How can I put those same principles to work in my life?*

It's easy to forget this country's greatness. Mostly we

seem to read and hear about what's gone *wrong*. That's partly due to the nature of the news media, which often focuses on the negative. Bad news sells. It's partly due to the fact that we Americans are a self-critiquing people. We're problem solvers, always driving to make things better. We draw attention to our nation's problems so we can fix them.

There's another reason it's easy to overlook America's greatness. Unfortunately these days, some people take the view that America is a severely flawed place. They see its history mainly as a long series of injustices: stealing land from Native Americans, fouling the environment, enslaving Africans, withholding rights from women, exploiting laborers, discriminating against people of color, and waging imperialist wars against the third world. Being proud of America and praising it as an incredible place is viewed as unsophisticated.

Shortchanging the American record is a shame because, first of all, it's simply wrong. Yes, the United States—like any other nation—has committed some grave wrongs and has some dark chapters in its past. Those chapters should of course be studied and their lessons learned. But a country, like a person, should be judged by the totality of its acts. In any honest assessment, America's record stands tall—tall enough to be called great.

It's also a shame because in focusing so much on the negative, a lot of people are casting away some real pearls of wisdom. They're losing sight of some great lessons and principles for building successful lives.

This book examines some principles on which America was founded, principles that conservatives admire and hold dear. (More about what the word *conservative* means a bit later.) These principles have made America great, and they can give you a running start in your own life.

Of course, a short book like this can't cover this topic completely. But we hope it will inspire your own study of America and the principles behind its achievement. Armed with that knowledge, you'll have some good tools to make your own unique contribution.

The American founders recognized the link between the life of this country and the kind of lives its citizens lead. A nation governed by the people depends on the wisdom, values, and choices of its citizens. As James Madison observed, democracy depends on virtues like industriousness, self-reliance, and respect. "Republican government presupposes the existence of these qualities in a higher degree than any other form" of government, he wrote.[1]

The success of this country depends on people like you. And in many ways, your success depends on the strength and greatness of this country. Your chances are all the better if you know what has made this country great and good. Its principles can help you make your way in the world of academics, work, family, and citizenship. They can help you take advantage of your liberty to build a life that is good and dedicated to high purpose.

APPRECIATING AMERICA'S GREATNESS

FROM ITS BEGINNING, the United States has been one of the most amazing countries in history. If you step back and look at the broad picture, you see just how remarkable the American record is.

- The United States was the first nation in history created out of the belief that people should govern themselves. The US Constitution is the oldest written constitution in operation. It has been a model for country after country as democracy has spread around the world.
- The US military is the greatest defender of freedom in the world. From the Revolutionary War to World War II to the fight against terrorism, American soldiers have stood for freedom. They have brought more liberty to

more people than any other military force in history.

- No other country has done a better job of establishing equal rights for all citizens. Certainly there have been times when the United States has fallen short of its founding principles. But especially in recent decades, no country has worked harder to eliminate discrimination and protect the rights of minorities. Simply put, this is one of the best countries in the world—if not *the* best— in which to be a minority.

- No other country has welcomed and united so many people from so many different shores. Never before have so many people from different backgrounds, races, nationalities, and religions lived and worked together so peacefully.

- American companies have made the United States one of the most powerful economic engines the world has known and one of the most prosperous countries in history. American companies provide some of the best jobs in the world. They've also built innumerable hospitals, libraries, and parks; created great universities; filled museums with works of art; found cures for diseases; and improved life in countless ways.

- The United States is the world's greatest marketplace for the free exchange of ideas and information. The staggering volume of information traded here every day—via books, newspapers, magazines, the Internet, TV, and radio—makes this the liveliest center of thought and debate in history.

- America is a world leader in scholarship and invention. It is home to the world's finest collection of universities and research institutions. The record of American inventions and discoveries goes on and on, from the mechanical reaper to the microchip.

- This country is the planet's largest source of humanitarian aid. Government programs and private giving make up one of the greatest efforts to help people in history. When disasters strike overseas, Americans are among the first to offer help and support.

This doesn't mean that Americans are better than everyone else, or that the United States is always right, or that the country is without faults. Of course it has many faults; its history includes wrongs such as slavery and segregation. All human institutions are imperfect. Yet over the years Americans have shown themselves to be pretty good at taking a hard look at the nation's wrongs and trying to make them right.

What makes this country truly exceptional are the promises and principles of America—the old truths written into the Declaration of Independence and the Constitution. Freedom of thought and speech. Equality before the law. The right to worship God as we please. The dignity of each individual. The freedom to pursue dreams and the opportunity to live to our fullest potential.

It's important to understand America's achievement—and to be unembarrassed to say that this is a great and good nation. Why?

First, because it is the truth, and the truth is always worth saying. If we forget the truth about this country's greatness, we stop being a great people. We weaken the American spirit.

Second, recognizing America's greatness helps make us grateful. No other country has ever offered so much opportunity to learn, to grow, to make a living, to make a mark. We can't take that for granted. Let us not commit the sin of ingratitude for so many blessings.

Third, recognizing America's goodness helps us appreciate and love this country. And loving it makes us want to protect it. Nothing good lasts when people don't cherish and protect it. If we don't stand up for America, it will disappear. It's up to all of us—you and me—to take care of this miraculous country, to keep it great, to love it.

Finally, appreciating this country's achievements can help you improve yourself. Think of it this way. Smart business executives study successful companies to sharpen their business skills. Athletes who want to win study successful teams. Getting to know some of the principles that have made your country great can improve your own chances of success.

CONSERVATIVE PRINCIPLES: AN OVERVIEW

THIS CHAPTER GIVES A BRIEF OVERVIEW of what it means to be a conservative. For a little more detail, look at the chapters in the rest of this book. There you'll find issue-by-issue answers to questions about conservative ideas and values.

The term *conservative* comes from the Latin word *conservare*, which means to keep safe, maintain, or preserve. Conservatives want to preserve society's best values and wisdom. In America, that includes some principles on which this country was founded and which have made this nation great.

Although there is no neat and tidy list of American conservative beliefs, there are several ideas that conservatives tend to agree with. One handy way to remember those ideas is the acronym FLINT, which corresponds to the five concepts of *Free enterprise*, *Limited government*,

Individual liberty, National defense, and *Traditional values.* These five concepts are critical for understanding American conservative thought.

Free Enterprise

Conservatives recognize that free enterprise—or capitalism, as it's also known—is the best system the world has ever known for creating jobs and good living conditions. It has lifted millions of people out of poverty and made their lives better.

The liberty we enjoy is closely connected to free enterprise. At its best, free enterprise makes possible the liberty we have to choose our own paths, to work toward our goals and dreams.

Free enterprise is by no means perfect. It can cause excessive materialism. Wide gaps can open between rich and poor. We'll always need sensible laws and people with good values to help keep our economic system free and fair.

Despite its drawbacks, the free enterprise system is without equal in giving people the opportunity to earn a good living. It is a cornerstone of our republic, our liberty, and our nation's success.

Limited Government

Limited government means government powerful enough to protect people's liberty and rights and vigorous enough to help make the country a better place but not so powerful that it keeps sticking its nose into people's business and stepping on their rights, liberties, and opportunities.

The American founders realized that over time governments have a natural tendency to assume greater power and exert more control over people. In framing the Constitution, the founders did their best to set up checks and balances to curb government's power.

Despite their efforts, today's federal government keeps growing, spending, borrowing, taxing, and regulating. It has run up a huge debt that threatens the country's future.

Conservatives recognize that government has important work to do, but they want to rein in its out-of-control growth and spending. More government is not the solution to every problem. Other institutions—such as families, neighborhoods, houses of worship, schools, and volunteer groups—are often the best places to solve problems and improve lives.

Individual Liberty

The Declaration of Independence states that all people are endowed by their creator with the right to liberty. That right does not come from the government. It is a gift from God. The government's job is to protect our liberty.

Most of the world's history is one of rule by kings, dictators, and governments that told people how they must live. That's still true today in many places. Liberty is very precious, and we must never take it for granted.

Liberty doesn't mean doing whatever we want without regard for others. That is licentiousness, a lack of moral restraint. True liberty comes with responsibilities. It involves a commitment to acting the right way. It means using our freedom to take charge of our conduct and owning up to it.

Liberty worth having requires virtues like self-restraint, honor, and respect for others. It involves living up to obligations. It involves thinking not just of self but of the common good.

National Defense

We owe our liberty and our existence as a country to the US military. It is the greatest defender of freedom in the world. There have been times when America has made mistakes with its armies and has even committed grave injustices. But overall the world is a much better place because of the American soldier, and it's a much safer place because our military is strong.

Defending the country from foreign attack is arguably the federal government's most important job. No other part of society is capable of taking over that responsibility.

We live in dangerous times. Maintaining a powerful military is not only the best way to defend ourselves; it's also the best way to keep the peace. It's an expensive obligation. But as General Douglas MacArthur once said, "The inescapable price of liberty is an ability to preserve it from destruction."

Traditional Values

When conservatives study human activity and history, they recognize certain truths that run through all time—principles about how best to live and how to treat our fellow human beings. Values like "love your neighbor as yourself" and "honesty is the best policy." Moral truths like "thou shalt not steal," as the Ten Commandments put it. Such standards of right and wrong are crucial to having a good life.

In America, being conservative also involves a commitment to principles on which this country was founded—ideals such as the belief that all people are created equal and that all have the right to think and speak freely. These traditional American principles have made the United States a powerful force for good in the world.

Conservatives don't claim to be morally superior to anyone else. Like everyone else, they are imperfect creatures. But they are concerned with preserving our best values and ways that help us live up to them.

Conservatives understand that culture shapes and reflects people's values. Music, art, books, movies, television shows, websites—they all send messages about right and wrong, acceptable and unacceptable behavior. It makes a big difference whether the culture is sending messages that marriage is a serious matter and that doing drugs is dangerous and wrong, or whether it sends messages that no one expects marriages to last and that smoking pot is fine. Traditional values have a hard time surviving if the culture is at war with them.

None of this means that conservatives don't like change or the modern world. It's true that they often look to the past for guidance. They want to preserve the best values and wisdom handed down through the centuries. But conservatives also look to the future. They are eager to embrace change that makes sense and is in line with good, sound values. After all, if we never change, we can never make ourselves better.

Conservatives are dedicated to these principles because they keep this country free, strong, and good. Conservatives also realize that these principles can help us all build successful lives.

Part 1

FREE ENTERPRISE

America is a prosperous nation because here you are free to profit from your own labor. You are free to put your talents and passions to work, to offer the best you can, to live to your fullest potential. You are blessed with the liberty and opportunity to raise yourself up. If you take advantage of that freedom with energy, dedication, and perseverance, you have a very good chance of sharing in this nation's success.

WORKING, STRIVING, ACHIEVING

Whatever career you choose, your work will be possible because of the free enterprise system. It's the engine that powers our nation's economy. Without it, the modern world as we know it would not exist.

Free enterprise is an economic system in which property, resources, and industry are controlled by individuals and businesses—not the government—to make profits. Another name for free enterprise is capitalism, although free enterprise is in many ways a more accurate term since the freedom to conduct business is one of its bedrock principles.

Free enterprise is more than being able to own your

own property or start a business, although those things are very important. It means the freedom to work hard at something you care about, to strive toward a goal you choose, and to achieve perhaps more than you once thought possible.

Is free enterprise good or bad for the world?

Free enterprise has its drawbacks, but overall it's a terrific economic system—the best the world has known. It's certainly the best system in history for creating jobs and material well-being.

One way to appreciate free enterprise is to look at what life was like before it came along. Modern free enterprise began in Great Britain along with the Industrial Revolution in the latter part of the eighteenth century. Before then, cities such as London were filthy, violent places where most people struggled simply to make it from one day to the next. Most people were illiterate. Poverty and disease were rampant. Jobs were hard to come by and often fleeting. The masses owned little more than the clothes on their backs.[1]

In the short term, free enterprise and industrialism did little to improve people's conditions—in some ways, they may have made things worse. You may have read Charles Dickens's descriptions of early industrial towns full of soot-covered streets and dark factories with chimneys "out of which interminable serpents of smoke trailed themselves for ever and ever, and never got uncoiled."[2]

But over time, as nations and cities adjusted to the upheaval brought on by rapid change, something close to miraculous happened. For millions of people, life got immeasurably better as they gained access to mass-produced goods—clothes, furniture, books, and automobiles. As business increased, so did job opportunities. A middle class emerged. Literacy spread. Incomes rose. People began to live much longer. Free enterprise was not solely responsible for these changes, but it had a great deal to do with them.

Yes, there is a troubling side to free enterprise. There are booms and busts. People get laid off, sometimes at the worst of times, as companies watch their bottom lines. In some parts of the world, workers labor in sweatshops.

But overall, the effects of free enterprise have improved people's lives in countless ways. It is difficult to imagine what life would be like without mass-produced computers, phones, lights, washers, medicines, vaccines, motors, pens, soap, tires—the list goes on and on.

Is free enterprise a moral system?

Critics say that free enterprise causes greed and excessive ambition. It turns life into a vicious competition in which the ruthless and dishonest exploit others to come out ahead.

In truth, sometimes people can and do act immorally in business—just as people sometimes act immorally in government or in their family lives. But we must weigh the good against the bad. All in all, free enterprise has done enormous good by creating better lives for billions of people.

That said, the main purpose of free enterprise is to help people prosper materially. To make sure people act morally and treat each other fairly in a free enterprise system, we have to look outside of free enterprise itself.

Government can help here. Laws that keep businesses from putting children to work or dumping chemicals in streams, for example, are good checks on free enterprise. As long as they don't hamper business with too much red tape, legislatures and courts can be business's allies in improving lives.

More important than government, though, is culture. The morality of any society's economic system depends on the morality of its culture. A corrupt culture will produce corrupt enterprise (and corrupt government). A decent culture will produce businesses that treat people well.

That means our most important institutions—families, churches and other houses of worship, neighborhoods, schools, and communities—must help produce people of good character who make good employers and employees. It takes a lot of work to maintain a culture that keeps capitalism within moral bounds. In a world full of commercialism, attention to virtue helps keep money and the things it can buy in perspective.

Calvin Coolidge, the thirtieth president of the United States, is famous for saying that "the chief business of the American people is business." But he also reminded us that for all the prosperity that free enterprise has brought this country, without dedication to some deeper matters, it's all for nothing. "The things of the spirit come first," he said. "Unless we cling to that, all our material prosperity, overwhelming though it may appear, will turn to a barren sceptre in our grasp."[3]

How can we accomplish good in the world of work?

We all want to make a good living. But we also want our work to help us make good lives.

Work can help us become better people because it encourages us to exercise virtues. In work we learn responsibility when given tasks. We gain perseverance in meeting tough deadlines. We learn how to complete big jobs by tackling small pieces. "Heaven is not reached at a single bound," as an old poem says.

Entrepreneurs exercise creativity in coming up with new ideas. They develop habits of thrift in saving to start a business and dedication in getting it off the ground. Managers and employees alike learn the value of honesty because the reality is that in the world of work, dishonesty is one of the surest ways to lose a business or to get fired.

Our work can also help make the world a better place. That's what most business owners do when they hire people or when they sell products that people need. It's what employees do when they make a product or provide a service well. They are helping others while they earn a living.

The man working on a road who does his best to

make it level is smoothing the way for others. A woman who buys produce for a grocery store chain is helping put food on families' tables. They both help move the world along.

A farmer was once driving a visitor across his land, and they came to a place where he had labored to plant acres of tree saplings that would someday be valuable timber. "You'll be dead and gone before they're ever harvested," his visitor commented. "Why put in a crop like that?" They crested a hill, and a stand of tall, thick trees stretched before them. "Because my father planted these for me," the farmer said.

No matter what our work, we can always choose to do it well and with others in mind, and that adds to the supply of universal good.

MAKING *the* MOST *of* OPPORTUNITIES

They do me wrong who say I come no more
When once I knock and fail to find you in;
For every day I stand outside your door
And bid you wake, and rise to fight and win.

WALTER MALONE

THIS VERSE, FROM THE OLD POEM "Opportunity," is about as American as a rhyme could be. The United States is the land of second, third, and fourth chances. That's one of the wonderful things about living here.

There are reasons why this country is a nation of fabulous opportunities. It's important to recognize those reasons, not only for your own success but also for keeping this country great.

What makes America the "land of opportunity"?

There is no single ingredient to the recipe. It's a mixture of several things.

The first is liberty, including economic freedom. That freedom allows people to choose their own careers and put their talents to work. It allows them to profit from their own ideas and labor and to work for themselves if they want to.

Abraham Lincoln said, "This progress by which the poor, honest, industrious, and resolute man raises himself, that he may work on his own account, and hire somebody else . . . is the great principle for which this government was really formed."[1]

Limited government that protects rights and freedoms is another important ingredient. For example, it is the government's job to protect property rights, keep markets as free and fair as possible, and oppose discrimination in the workplace. Too much government, on the other hand, weighs down the economy with high taxes and costly regulations. That kills opportunity for individuals and businesses.

National character is a third ingredient. The American spirit values business. It prizes inventiveness, entrepreneurship, and hard work. It also values education—Americans have always believed that education and opportunity go together.

The moral character of the American people is crucial—composed of virtues like dealing honestly with others, wanting to do good work, and taking personal responsibility. Where those virtues don't exist, opportunity doesn't last.

Families make a big difference. Family is the first and most important teacher of the character needed for success. It's where we first learn the virtues that make a healthy work ethic, virtues such as integrity, dedication, and perseverance. Talk to people who have had success, and they often say things like "My dad taught me to never quit" or "My mom made me believe I could do it."

Finally, strong communities are essential. Vibrant neighborhoods, churches, and civic groups like the local chamber of commerce or Lions Club are places where opportunity thrives. They form networks where you can look for jobs, build a reputation, and develop business relationships. These institutions, plus families, are the backbone of American opportunity.

What does the "pursuit of happiness" mean?

The Declaration of Independence says we are all endowed by our Creator with the right to "life, liberty, and the pursuit of happiness." What did the founders mean by that phrase? Is happiness something we're supposed to chase and catch?

In this case, "happiness" doesn't mean being cheerful or feeling good. We have to look to other sources to help us decipher exactly what the Declaration is getting at here. To understand it, we need to turn to the ancient Greeks, whom Thomas Jefferson and the other founders had studied.

The Greek word for happiness was *eudaimonia*, which includes the idea of personal well-being or flourishing. To the Greeks, being happy meant living a good life, not just in the sense of being comfortable and safe and having nice things but also in living a virtuous life. A person can't be truly happy without virtues such as self-control, honesty, and courage.

The ancient Greeks also connected happiness with fulfilling one's potential. A good lyre player, for example, is happy when playing the lyre well. A computer scientist is happy working with computers, and a businessman is happy making business deals. In other words, one's chosen work can bring happiness—whether it's paying work, volunteer work, or work at being a father or mother.

The idea of the American Dream is connected to the idea of the pursuit of happiness. The American Dream means much more than owning a house, a car, and a big flat-screen TV. It means the chance to follow a dream, to work hard at turning a vision into something real.

If Jefferson were alive today, he might say that "the pursuit of happiness" is something like the opportunity to reach one's fullest potential. The Declaration says we all have the God-given right to use our abilities to go as far as we can. There is no guarantee of a good life, but in America there is the opportunity to strive for one morally, intellectually, and economically.

How do we take advantage of the opportunities this country offers?

Despite its problems, this country still offers more opportunity for success than any other nation on earth. That's one big reason to be grateful for being an American: we have opportunities here that people in other countries can only dream of.

It's also true that in no other country are opportunity and work more connected. Thomas Edison, who represents one of the greatest success stories of all time, knew that. People called him a wizard because of the stream of inventions that came from his laboratories. "Wizard?" he replied. "Pshaw. It's plain hard work that does it."[2]

There is no surefire formula for success, but there is a pretty good plan that usually increases people's opportunities over the long term. It's a prescription for getting ahead called the "success sequence." Social scientists, economists, and people with common sense have known about it for a long time. Follow these steps in the right order, and your chances of getting ahead are good.

Here's the sequence: 1) Finish high school. A college degree is even better, but at least finish high school. 2) Get a job. It doesn't have to be a dream job you'll have forever—simply a full-time job, one you're qualified for. 3) Get married. Yes, marriage is good for financial success. 4) Have babies and start to raise them *after* you get married.

That's it. Get an education, get a job, get married, and start a family, in that order. If everybody in America followed this path, studies show that the poverty rate would plummet.[3] Stick to that sequence, and you vastly increase your access to the American Dream.

This solution calls for personal responsibility. Following the "success sequence" is easier said than done—steps like finishing a degree and getting a job are big ones. They take perseverance. Keeping a marriage healthy and raising children are even bigger challenges. But if more Americans will get back to following that route, this country will still be the land of opportunity.

BEING *a* GOOD STEWARD

IN ONE OF HIS FAMOUS PARABLES, Jesus tells the story of a man who summons three servants and puts them in charge of his property before traveling abroad. When he returns, he discovers that two of the servants have put his money to good use and made a handsome profit. He rewards them with greater responsibility. The third servant, fearful of losing the money in his charge, has simply buried it so he can return it to his master exactly as he received it. He ends up losing his job.[1]

The parable contains several good lessons, not the least of which is this: we should always try to put the gifts we have received to good use. How we put our God-given talents to use in earning a living matters. What we do with the money we earn also matters.

Is it wrong to want to make lots of money?

As long as you do it honestly, there's nothing wrong with making lots of money. Free enterprise rewards people with money for putting their talents, energy, and ideas to work.

It's important to recognize that there is a good side to people's ambitions for wealth. For example, that ambition is a big reason new products are invented, from automobiles and airplanes to computers and cell phones. Such inventions drive civilization forward and improve lives around the world.

An engineer who builds her own firm may end up making a lot of money, and a desire for wealth may be one of the reasons she founds her company. But along the way, that firm can provide good jobs for its employees and services for its clients.

The real question is, What do you do with your money? How do you handle it?

Jesus said it is easier for a camel to pass through the

eye of a needle than for a rich man to enter the Kingdom of Heaven.[2] The image is a powerful reminder of the dangers wealth can bring.

Jesus wasn't saying that rich people are bad. But he was telling us that riches can lead to real problems. Often the more a person has, the more he or she thinks about material possessions. It's easy to become wrapped up in wealth and lose sight of the truly important things in life.

Jesus was also reminding us that more money brings greater responsibilities. The rich have a choice to spend selfishly or generously. They can think of their money as theirs alone, or they can regard it as an obligation to practice good stewardship of God's bounty.

At its best, free enterprise creates wealthy people who use their wealth to serve others. Those who make lots of money do well to recall, as the apostle Paul tells us, that "God loveth a cheerful giver."[3]

As for those among us who don't make lots of money, it's good to remember that free enterprise offers the best opportunity to rise in the world and to make more money. If we do it right, we can help others along the way.

Do free enterprise and protecting the environment go together?

Hollywood films and news reports often present the view that free enterprise is a natural enemy of the environment. It's not uncommon for them to portray businesspeople as caring only about making money. Sometimes they go out of their way to imply that conservatives in particular don't care about the earth.

It's an absurd claim. In truth, conservatives care about the environment as much as anyone else. *Conservation* and *conservatism* share the same Latin root *conservare*, meaning to preserve and keep safe.

Unlike radical environmentalists, conservatives don't believe that human activity is essentially bad for the planet. They support good stewardship of the earth while putting its resources to work in smart, efficient ways that benefit people.

Environmentalism has done much good for the world. There are people who are willing to despoil the earth for personal gain, and sensible laws are certainly necessary to help protect the environment. Yet some environmentalists are so zealous, they forget to take people's well-being into account.

Their views about energy are a good example. Radical environmentalists are up in arms about oil wells and oil pipelines. They condemn drilling for natural gas, especially hydraulic fracking. They don't like coal-burning plants, even ones that use clean coal technology. They oppose construction of nuclear plants. But people need energy, and without any of those options we'd all be in very bad shape.

People in poor, developing countries especially need such energy. More than 1.2 billion people around the world lack access to electricity. Another 2.8 billion use fuels like wood, charcoal, and animal dung to cook—fuels that have negative health and environmental consequences.[4] Access to energy sources like oil and natural gas means better lives for much of the world's poor.

Conservatives believe that free enterprise, used wisely, can go hand in hand with preserving the environment. New technologies made possible by free enterprise can be used to solve environmental problems. For example, improved auto technology has reduced tailpipe emissions by 95 percent since 1970.[5]

The book of Genesis lays down an excellent principle when it says that "the LORD God took the man and put him in the Garden of Eden to work it and take care of it."[6] We are all charged with the stewardship of God's creation. That means watching over the earth. It also means working it in ways that put its bounty to good use. As is so often the case in life, balance is needed between those two goals.

Part 2

LIMITED GOVERNMENT

Independence lies at the core of the American character. After all, this country started with a Declaration of Independence. The American founders realized that without some measure of independence and self-reliance, no one can be truly happy. They envisioned a nation of people who looked not to a king, dictator, or big government bureaucracy for their security, but to themselves. If you want to be successful, you have to take charge of your own life.

TAKING CHARGE *of* OUR LIVES *and* OUR GOVERNMENT

*Ours was the first revolution in the history
of mankind that truly reversed the course of
government, and with three little words: "We
the People." "We the People" tell the government
what to do; it doesn't tell us. "We the People" are
the driver; the government is the car. And we
decide where it should go, and by what route,
and how fast. Almost all the world's constitutions
are documents in which governments tell the
people what their privileges are. Our Constitution
is a document in which "We the People"
tell the government what it is allowed to do.*

Those words, spoken by President Ronald Reagan as he left office in 1989, are a good, simple explanation of the idea of limited government. It's the kind of government the American founders set up in the United States Constitution. They wanted a country where people could take charge of their own lives.

Today a lot of people want another kind of government. They're in the habit of thinking that whenever someone has a problem, government should have a solution. It's a notion that calls on government to fix every leaky faucet in life. In the process, government takes more control of people's lives.

What kind of government is best for America, limited government or leaky-faucet government? The answer determines what kind of country you're going to live in—and the kind of life you see for yourself.

What does "limited government" mean?

Limited government is government restricted in power. It's powerful enough to protect people's God-given rights and liberty. It's energetic enough to help make the country a better place. But it's not so powerful that it threatens our rights and squelches opportunity.

The country's founders tried hard to restrict the government's power with the checks and balances they built into the system, like giving the president power to veto bills passed by Congress. They also tried to make sure that power would be divided between the federal and state governments.

Why did the founders want to limit government? They were students of human nature and history. They knew that there are people who love to wield power over others. As Samuel Adams put it, "Ambition and lust of power above the law are . . . predominant passions in the breasts of most men."[1]

The founders also knew that over time, governments have a tendency to amass power. For most of the world's history, after all, people had lived under rulers who grabbed all the power they could get.

If government's power is unrestricted, it will naturally grow and control more of people's lives. According to Thomas Jefferson, "The natural progress of things is for liberty to yield, and government to gain ground."[2]

Unfortunately, that's exactly what has happened in this country. The federal government in Washington, DC, keeps amassing more and more power. Federal bureaucracies issue thousands of new regulations every year, affecting everything from the clothes we wear to the schools we attend.

Some of the government's expansion is due simply to the growth of the country, but much has come from the government taking more power for itself, just as the founders feared. Many officials in Washington think they know better than people living in places like Iowa and Alabama. They believe they should wield power because they have superior wisdom and expertise.

In truth, there is no special wisdom that comes from being in Washington, DC. Living in the nation's capital doesn't make you smarter or more knowledgeable than Americans elsewhere. Yet a "we know what's best for you" mind-set is often the way the federal government acts.

What's so bad about big government?

The federal government is so huge and bloated, it creates all sorts of problems.

- **Big government is wildly expensive.** Washington spends a massive amount of money. In 2014, for example, it spent about $3.5 trillion. It borrowed about fourteen cents out of every dollar spent.[3]

It has racked up $19 trillion in debt as of 2016, a number that keeps rising. That comes to nearly $60,000 of debt for every American.[4] No one knows how that money will be repaid.

- **Bureaucracy is often inefficient and wasteful.** Stories of government waste are so common, people barely notice them anymore—we are inundated by reports of the government spending billions of dollars on programs that don't work as advertised and that end up costing three or four times more than promised.

- **Fraud and abuse can be a big problem.** For example, Medicare and Medicaid—huge programs that pay for health care for the elderly and the poor—have rampant problems with health care providers overbilling the government. No one even knows how much abuse is involved. It may be $100 billion a year or more.[5]

- **Many programs keep going even if they don't work well or at all.** Head Start, a preschool program for children in low-income families, is a good example. Its goal is a good one: to help children in low-income families get ready for elementary school. But according to a study released by the US Department of Health and Human Services, the program has no lasting effects on children's achievement in school.[6]

- **Big government can stifle the economy.** Many times government officials simply do not appreciate the burden that having too many laws and regulations puts on businesses—especially small businesses, which are the backbone of the American economy. Dealing with excessive regulation costs time and money. It slows business and chokes opportunities. Many small businesses say that government regulations have become one of the biggest obstacles to their growth.

- **Big government poses risks to freedom.** This may be the most damaging effect of all. Government is so big that it has something to say about virtually every aspect of our lives. Federal rules determine how much water our toilets use and what kind of lightbulbs we screw into our lamps. They dictate what kind of ingredients go into our food and what kind of mileage our cars get.

Laws are necessary, of course. They help make sure the meat we buy is safe and our rivers are clean. But the larger and more powerful government becomes, the more control it has over our lives. The question is, where do we cross the line from being the land of the free to becoming a land of government decree?

How do I take part in government of the people, by the people, for the people?

The first thing to do is stay informed. It takes a little time, but not as much as you may think. Start by simply paying attention when the news comes on the radio or TV. Take a little spare time to read online reports or a newspaper. Most people, once they start paying attention to current events, enjoy keeping up. They even become passionate about an issue or two.

You don't have to become an expert in current affairs. Simply keep your ears and eyes open. It's shocking how many Americans stay so little informed. Many can't name their own congressman or senators. (Can you?) You can't make intelligent decisions without some information.

Knowing some history makes you better informed too. Pick up a book about Columbus's voyage or George

Washington's life or the flight of Apollo 11. American history is full of great, entertaining stories.

The more you know about this country's past, the more you'll appreciate what a rare, wonderful place America is. Knowing some history helps you understand why the founders insisted on limited government and what we mean by "government of the people, by the people, and for the people." (Do you know where that phrase comes from? If not, do a quick Internet search and find out. It's from one of the country's most precious documents and famous events.)

It should go without saying, but it still needs to be said since so many people fail to do it: when election time comes, you need to vote. Someone once pointed out that bad government is elected by good citizens who don't bother to vote. Don't be taken in by cynics who say your vote doesn't matter. It *does* matter, in part because it's your solemn obligation as a citizen.

Before you vote, ask yourself some hard questions. Do the promises the candidate is making really make good common sense? Is another government program really the solution? Is it likely to make a difference or just be a waste of money? How much is it going to cost? Who's going to pay for it?

When people vote without asking these questions, they're probably just voting themselves more big, bloated government. And that means giving government more control over their lives.

BEING SELF-RELIANT

THE STORY OF DAVID AND GOLIATH is one of the world's all-time greatest stories of faith and self-reliance. When David faced Goliath, he put his faith in God. But he also had to trust himself. He had to rely on his own skill and courage.

Before David went out to meet Goliath, King Saul offered the young man his own sword and armor, but David declined, explaining that he was not skilled in their use. He knew that each individual must fight his own battles with his own weapons. He went forth carrying his staff, his shepherd's bag, his sling, and five smooth stones—all he would need to defeat Goliath.

There are many times in life when we need to rely on our own resources to overcome obstacles. A strong sense of self-reliance has traditionally been an important part of the American character. It's one of the traits that has made this country great.

Is it a good idea to rely on the government for our needs?

Over the last several decades the federal government has been steadily growing, promising to take care of more and more of people's needs. In many ways the United States has become a "welfare state," a country in which government assumes large responsibility for people's well-being, including their financial needs.

The American welfare state has grown into a vast network of agencies that administer hundreds of programs delivering money, goods, and services to millions of people. Some programs are truly needed and can make a real difference. But is it smart to expect the government to take care of many responsibilities for us?

One problem with the welfare state is that it often fails to solve problems. Take, for example, the effort to fight poverty. Since the 1960s, government has spent more than $20 trillion to help the poor—a goal we all share. Yet for all that spending, the poverty rate has not changed much. Rather than lifting people out of poverty, the programs have left generations dependent on government aid.[1]

An overreaching welfare state has some serious downsides for all Americans, rich and poor. It weakens the American character. As the government takes more and more charge of people's well-being, people come to expect problems to be solved for them. That undermines personal responsibility.

It can also undermine the spirit of work. If people don't have to work, many will choose not to. This is human nature. When big government sends the message "You will be taken care of" and then follows that message with years of entitlement benefits, it can erode people's desire to earn their own living. It's no coincidence that as the welfare state has expanded, many people have stopped working.[2]

The more the government does for us, the more we come to rely on it. It creates dependency while destroying self-reliance. It can even create among people a sense that they are entitled to government payouts and services.

President Franklin Roosevelt, who in many ways

launched the American welfare state during the Great Depression, recognized the dangers of dependency on government. He said that "continued dependence upon relief induces a spiritual and moral disintegration fundamentally destructive to the national fibre. To dole out relief in this way is to administer a narcotic, a subtle destroyer of the human spirit."[3]

Why is self-reliance important?

Aesop, in one of his fables, tells how a wagoner was driving his team along a road after a hard rain when his wheels got stuck deep in the mud. He climbed down from his wagon, stood there a few minutes cursing his bad luck, and called out for Hercules to come help him.

After a while the famous hero appeared and said to him, "Put your shoulder to the wheel, man, and urge your horses forward, and then you may call on me to assist you. If you won't lift a finger to help yourself, you can't expect anyone else to come to your aid." The farmer pushed with all his might, the wagon moved forward, and pretty soon he was riding along again with the knowledge that self-help is the best help.

Self-reliance is a very American ideal. This country

was founded on it. The Declaration of Independence, after all, was an announcement that the American colonists were determined to stand on their own.

Of course, you can't get through life all on your own. There are plenty of times when we genuinely need others' help. Most of those times, it makes sense to turn to people closest to us—family members, friends, neighbors, and members of our house of worship. Sometimes we turn to community organizations—local associations, charities, businesses, civic clubs, and so on.

Government can help too, but Washington, DC, or the state capital shouldn't be the first place we automatically turn to. If we do, we're likely to be disappointed. Distant, faceless bureaucracies usually aren't the best solution. Their intentions may be good, but as a general rule, the farther away help is coming from, the less effective it's likely to be.

Politicians in Washington, DC, often promise a lot. But the results more often than not fall short of those promises. If you wait around for Washington to solve your problems for you, you're probably going to wait a long time.

Self-reliance is still an unbeatable problem solver and weapon for meeting life's misfortunes. As the American essayist Ralph Waldo Emerson once wrote, "The best lightning rod for your protection is your own spine."[4]

How do we best help those in need?

Conservatives are against the idea of a welfare state that shepherds people through life with government programs. But they also believe that America should use its vast resources to help those in real need. Here are a few principles that conservatives hold to when it comes to government helping others.

- **Aid should be focused on those who truly need it.** Government can provide a safety net to help catch those who have fallen on hard times and those who are unable to care for themselves. But it can't keep promising more and more benefits for more and more people. That will bankrupt the country.

- **Government programs must always encourage personal responsibility.** Government should not send the message that it can take care of all needs or protect people from all hardship or misfortune in life, because it can't.

- **Government benefits should not be designed to last forever.** Some programs, such as those that help the elderly or permanently disabled, must provide long-term help. But generally speaking, programs should be designed to help those in need get back on their feet and off government assistance as soon as possible, not trap them in a state of dependency.
- **When appropriate, programs should require people to work.** This applies, in particular, to welfare programs for low-income people. One of the best ways to get and keep people off welfare is to require them to work full-time in return for aid. Full-time work is also the best way for people to climb out of poverty.
- **We must do everything we can to strengthen families.** The decline of the two-parent family is a major cause of problems in this country. When families are strong, people have a much better chance of overcoming the problems they face.

Government should not be the first place people look to for help. Conservatives believe it should be a last resort. That belief brings with it a responsibility to step up and help those in need with personal action and giving. In other words, we shouldn't wait for government to help others. We should offer it ourselves—through churches, temples, neighborhood associations, charities, civic clubs, or volunteer groups. The best kind of help is given with our own hands.

HANDLING
OUR NATION'S
FINANCES WISELY

WHEN ABRAHAM LINCOLN was a young man living in the frontier village of New Salem, Illinois, he decided to go into business as a general storekeeper. In the process, he took on more debt than he could handle. Pretty soon the store "winked out," as Lincoln put it, leaving him owing creditors a huge amount of money.

He struggled for years to pay off what he half-jokingly called his "national debt." Others in his situation fled for the western territories to avoid paying, but Lincoln insisted on settling his debts. It wasn't easy—at one point his personal property was repossessed—but he finally succeeded. For the rest of his life, he was more careful about his finances. It was the last time he let himself into that kind of debt.

Finances matter, both for individuals and for countries. They matter a lot. The government's taxing and spending policies have a tremendous effect on the nation's well-being. And they very much affect how much money we have in our pockets. All of us—including the government—can take a lesson from Abraham Lincoln.

Why is high government debt wrong?

For years, the federal government has been spending more money than it has. It has piled up an enormous mountain of debt—$19 trillion and rising as of 2016.

That's roughly $60,000 of debt for each man, woman, and child in this country. That doesn't even include debts that state and local governments have racked up.[1]

If you want to see how fast the debt is mounting, go to the US National Debt Clock website (http://www.usdebtclock.org) and take a look. You won't like what you see.

What's causing so much national debt? One word: spending. Uncle Sam is like a man with a credit card on a spending spree. He keeps charging more and more things, but he doesn't have the money to pay for them.

Almost every year during the last few decades, the federal government has spent more money than it gets in taxes. Each year, it has to borrow money to make up for the deficit and cover all its bills.

The amount the government borrows varies from year to year, depending on the deficit. In 2014, it borrowed fourteen cents out of every dollar spent.[2]

As the nation's debt gets out of control, all sorts of bad things can happen. The government may eventually hike taxes to help pay for all its borrowing and spending. A huge debt could force the government to make deep cuts to many programs. It could also lead to inflation and higher interest rates.

All of these things would slow economic growth and weaken job markets, perhaps for a long time. The debt could put the American Dream at risk for rising generations.

Is debt going to throw the United States into financial ruin tomorrow? No. But twenty or thirty years down the road, it could cause serious economic problems.

That's why young people—students or recent graduates, for example—should be especially alarmed over government debt. If you are young, the burden is going to fall on you. You'll have to pay, one way or another, for all the spending and borrowing that is going on today.

Conservatives believe that the federal government has got to put the brakes on its out-of-control spending. It is wrong—both financially and morally—to burden rising generations with so much debt.

Are taxes good or bad?

In just a few years, if not sooner, you'll get your first full-time job. When that first paycheck comes, you'll probably be a little dismayed to find that a good chunk of your hard-earned salary goes to the government. Social security, Medicare, federal income taxes, state income taxes, maybe local income taxes, and more.

It leaves a lot of Americans asking themselves, *Where on earth is my money going? Is this a good or bad thing?*

Some taxes are necessary, of course. We must pay them to have a functioning government. As Justice Oliver Wendell Holmes put it more than a hundred years ago, "Taxes are what we pay for civilized society."[3]

That said, it's also true that in recent decades government has been gobbling up more and more money.

Many Americans feel like every time they turn around, they're hit with higher taxes.

High taxes are bad because they take money out of the hands of people and businesses that would otherwise be using it to buy things, make things, provide services, and hire workers—in other words, all the activities required to make the economy go.

High taxes also hurt individual freedom. The more the government takes in taxes, the more control it has, and the less freedom you have to use that money the way you want.

Every year, the Tax Foundation calculates Tax Freedom Day, the day when the United States as a whole has earned enough money to pay its tax bill. It's a handy way to understand how much of the nation's income goes to taxes.

In 2015, Tax Freedom Day came on April 24. For the first 113 days of the year—nearly a third of the calendar—America was working for the government, so to speak. Beginning April 24, we got to work for ourselves and our families.[4]

People who want to raise taxes should answer this question: Exactly how much of the year should we have to work for the government?

Why can't rich people pay all the taxes?

It's a tempting idea. Just let super-rich people pay all of our taxes for us—multibillionaires like Bill Gates (founder of Microsoft), Warren Buffett (the country's most famous investor), and Larry Page and Sergey Brin (founders of Google).

The problem is that even the super rich don't have enough money to pay the nation's tax bill year after year. In 2014, for example, Bill Gates was worth around $80 billion. The federal government spent about $3.5 trillion that year.[5] That means the government could seize all of Bill Gates's wealth and would get only *one forty-fourth* of the money needed to cover its expenses that year. Pretty soon it would run out of fortunes to seize.

What about people who aren't super rich but still make a lot of money? Can't they pay all the taxes for the rest of us?

In fact, they already do pay a huge portion of the nation's annual tax bill. Just 5 percent of all taxpayers make $176,000 or more a year, but that top 5 percent pays nearly 60 percent of all federal income taxes paid by the American people.[6]

The Bible tells us that of those to whom much is given, much is asked.[7] That's an important truth to remember. But it's also important to remember, perhaps with some gratitude, that high earners do carry a big part of the tax burden in this country. Much is asked of them, and they do give.

There's another reason it's a bad idea to take the attitude that someone else should pay the taxes. We all have a stake in this country. We all share its blessings. We should want to share in the responsibility of keeping it going. That means, in part, paying taxes.

Of course, some people don't make much money. They can't pay much, if anything, in taxes. That's understandable. But in a prosperous nation like the United States, the majority of Americans should be able to help foot the bill.

Part 3

INDIVIDUAL LIBERTY

This nation has flourished by protecting people's God-given right to liberty. You, as an American, are blessed with the freedom to set your own goals and strive for them. A good life entails using freedom in responsible ways. To be truly successful, you have to look at your liberty not just in terms of doing what you want but also in terms of the obligations that freedom brings.

LIVING UP *to* OUR RESPONSIBILITIES

WE OFTEN TAKE OUR LIBERTY FOR GRANTED. It's easy to think, *Of course I'm free to say what I think and to worship however I want.*

That's a mistake, however, because the liberties we Americans enjoy are fragile blessings. Much of the world does not have such freedom. Liberty always needs protecting. *Always.* "Eternal vigilance is the price of liberty," an old saying goes. It's absolutely true.

We must remember that liberty walks hand in hand with responsibility. American freedom rests on the idea that most people are capable of being responsible for their own affairs and should be. Every time we don't take responsibility for our own affairs and instead place that responsibility in government's hands, we give up some of our freedom.

What are the duties that come with our liberty?

For each liberty we enjoy, there are corresponding responsibilities we need to uphold. For example, the freedom to own property comes with a responsibility to care for it. If you let a building you own get so run down that it becomes a danger to others, government is likely to fine you or condemn the building.

The freedom to own a gun (guaranteed by the Second Amendment) works only when people take extreme care in how they use one. Those who use a gun irresponsibly or to commit a crime lose their right to have one.

Free speech involves taking responsibility for what we say and write so that we don't harm others with our words. It also comes with the responsibility to respect others' right to state their beliefs freely. Sometimes we may disagree with their beliefs, but that doesn't mean we can demand they keep silent. Being able to state unpopular opinions is, in many ways, the essence of free speech.

In the days of ancient Greece, the young men of Athens took an oath to their city around age seventeen or eighteen. The Athenian Oath is still a good model to remind us of some basic civic duties that help uphold freedom. It went like this:

> We will never bring disgrace on this our City
> by an act of dishonesty or cowardice.
>   We will fight for the ideals and Sacred
> Things of the City both alone and with many.
>   We will revere and obey the City's laws,
> and will do our best to incite a like reverence
> and respect in those above us who are prone
> to annul them or set them at naught.
>   We will strive increasingly to quicken the
> public's sense of civic duty.
>   Thus in all these ways we will transmit this
> City, not only not less, but greater and more
> beautiful than it was transmitted to us.[1]

That last sentence in particular is worth thinking about. In some way, however small, we all have a duty to leave our community, our state, and our country better off than before.

What is our responsibility under the "rule of law"?

The rule of law is the principle that law should govern a nation, not the wishes of kings, dictators, or government officials. Its opposite is the "rule of men." That's when rulers set themselves above the law and issue commands as they see fit, often in their own interests, not in the interests of the people.

When well-written laws are the authority of the land, people can expect their government to operate in fair, predictable ways. On the other hand, when officials have the power to make up and change rules as they go along, anything can happen. Freedom is usually the first casualty. Individual liberty can't survive for long when government has unrestrained power to say "do this" and "don't do that."

Likewise, liberty suffers when people lose respect for the law. A community or country where people don't obey the law is a place where no one is free to feel safe, own property, or live without their rights being violated.

Abraham Lincoln knew that reverence for the law is crucial in a free nation. "Let every American, every lover of liberty, every well wisher to his posterity, swear by the blood of the Revolution, never to violate in the least particular, the laws of the country; and never to tolerate their violation by others," he wrote. "Let every man remember that to violate the law, is to trample on the blood of his father, and to tear the character of his own, and his children's liberty."[2]

The rule of law is a big reason that millions of people around the world want to live in or do business in the United States. They believe they can count on the United States being a place where most people obey the law, where property rights are respected, and where authorities help protect against lawbreakers.

Those conditions do not exist in many other parts of the world—and some of those places can be a living hell. Liberty and justice exist here only as long as we take seriously our responsibilities to uphold the law.

KEEPING *a* SOUND MIND *and* BODY

A LOT OF PEOPLE IN THIS COUNTRY are jumping on a bandwagon that supports legalizing marijuana. A few states have already legalized pot, and other states are considering it.

Most people don't realize that even as this movement grows, the scientific evidence about the dangers of marijuana is piling up. As more people use marijuana, the harm to society and individual lives is piling up too.

Some people view using marijuana or other illegal drugs as a question of personal liberty. "It's my body," they say. "I should have the freedom to decide what to put in it."

That argument forgets that true liberty involves responsibilities to others. Many things you do in life affect your family, friends, and community. The question isn't simply, am I free to do this? but also, is it right and good that I do this?

The "I should be free to do what I want with my body" argument also overlooks reality. Getting involved with illegal drugs brings the risk of becoming enslaved to drugs. It makes you *less* free.

Isn't pot harmless?

There is a widespread myth that marijuana has no bad side effects, that it just makes you feel good. Before you buy into that myth, there are some things you should know.

Marijuana in the United States today is several times stronger than the marijuana people smoked in the 1970s and 1980s. Back then, marijuana was about 3 to 5 percent tetrahydrocannabinol (THC), the main psychoactive ingredient. The THC levels of today's marijuana average around 13 percent but can be more than 20 percent.[1]

That means today's pot is a much more powerful drug. And it leads to many more health risks:

- **Marijuana can cause permanent, long-term damage to the brain in young people.** Regular use can alter brain structure and function in ways that affect a host of mental activities, from memory to appetite to pleasure response and pain tolerance. Regular use can decrease your motivation to work hard in school or on the job. Studies show that it can also actually lower your IQ.[2]
- **Marijuana can harm the lungs and heart.** According to the American Lung Association, it contains thirty-three cancer-causing chemicals. Its smoke deposits tar in the lungs. Research links its use with the potential for heart attacks and other serious cardiovascular threats.[3]
- **Marijuana use increases the risk of mental illness.** Those illnesses include psychosis, schizophrenia, anxiety, and depression in adulthood. "The link between cannabis and

psychosis is quite clear now; it wasn't 10 years ago," says a prominent British neurobiologist.[4]

- **The short-term impact on judgment, coordination, and motor skills can be deadly.** More and more, marijuana is involved in fatal car crashes. Several researchers estimate that a driver has twice the risk of an automobile accident if there is any measurable amount of THC in the bloodstream.[5]

Marijuana users are fond of saying that it's not addictive. That's false. While most people who try marijuana will not become addicted—just like most people who drink aren't addicted to alcohol—some users do become addicts. "There is no question that marijuana can be addictive; that argument is over," says a medical expert at the National Institute on Drug Abuse.[6]

There is also no question that for some users, marijuana is a "gateway drug" to even worse narcotics like cocaine and heroin. Not all marijuana users will go on to harder drugs, but almost all users of harder drugs started with marijuana.[7]

Another myth says that marijuana is a medical miracle, good for treating all sorts of ailments from cancer to HIV. It is true that some patients with serious illnesses report that marijuana can help ease pain. But the idea that it can be used to treat a long list of diseases is not true. As the American Medical Association puts it, "Cannabis is a dangerous drug and as such is a public health concern."[8]

Is using illegal drugs immoral?

This may be the most important question to ask about drugs. Unfortunately, it's a question that doesn't get talked about enough these days.

Using illegal drugs is obviously wrong in that it's breaking the law. But the question of right and wrong goes much deeper than that.

The late political scientist James Q. Wilson summed it up this way: "Drug use is wrong because it is immoral and it is immoral because it enslaves the mind and destroys the soul."[9] Drug use is wrong because of what it does to human character. It destroys people's moral sense, and it makes them less than they should be by burning away their sense of responsibility. The whole point of taking illegal drugs, after all, is to suspend reality, at least for a while. That includes suspending moral obligations.

People addicted to drugs neglect their duties. The lure can become so strong that they will do nothing else but take drugs. They will neglect everything in life that is important, noble, and worthwhile for the sake of drugs. Drugs can make people bad family members and friends. They can make people disappoint and crush those who care about them. People addicted to drugs are bad employees and colleagues because drugs hurt their ability to give their best effort and be dependable.

Drugs can make people bad citizens by destroying the civic virtues that a free society depends on, virtues like self-reliance, honesty, and individual responsibility. No self-governing society can function when its citizens are in a drug-induced haze. Buying illegal drugs also aids drug cartels, evil people, and enemies of our country.

Using drugs neglects and disappoints God. It's no way to treat our bodies, which are his creation.

When people forget that this is a moral issue, when they neglect to see right and wrong, they let down their guard, and that's when they get into trouble with drugs. Then they pay dearly.

TREATING OTHERS
AS WE WOULD HAVE
THEM TREAT US

IN THE GOSPEL OF LUKE, Jesus tells one of his most famous parables, the story of the Good Samaritan. A traveler on the road from Jerusalem to Jericho is attacked by bandits and left half-dead. First a priest and then a Levite pass by without helping, but a man from Samaria tends to the traveler's wounds, takes him to an inn, and pays for his care.[1]

To fully appreciate the parable, it's important to understand that in Jesus' time, there was a great deal of hostility and mistrust between Jews and the people of Samaria, a region north of Judea. A Samaritan was the last person a Jewish audience would expect to be the hero of a story. Jesus was asking his listeners to think of the Samaritan not according to ethnicity or class but as a fellow human being.

The story has always resonated in America, perhaps in part because ours is a country filled with people of so many different ethnicities and backgrounds. Perhaps it also resonates because here in the United States, we have a remarkable amount of freedom in choosing how we treat others.

In many ways, the themes of the Good Samaritan parable have been a main story line running through United States history. Do we deal with each other according to race, class, or ethnicity? Or do we see each other as fellow Americans and human beings?

Is the United States a racist, oppressive place?

"America is still a deeply racist country." "Legal racism is gone, but it doesn't matter because racism is entrenched in every part of American life." "People who oppose President Obama just can't stand the color of his skin."

Sometimes you'll hear and read these kinds of statements in the news. Conservatives don't buy them. They know their country is a lot better than that.

Yes, bigotry and racism still exist among Americans of all colors. Sometimes shameful incidents of racism break into the news, and they're always widely denounced. They're denounced because racist views aren't representative of the country as a whole—of conservatives, liberals, Democrats, or Republicans.

Yes, this country has some chapters in its past that include the terrible treatment of some groups. Racism was once widespread throughout white America. Its effects devastated millions of lives.

But America today is not the America of fifty, one hundred, or two hundred years ago. No other country has done more to secure the rights and liberties of minorities. In today's America, people generally treat each other with respect and fairness—much more so than in many other parts of the world. The vast majority of Americans want nothing but the best for their fellow Americans.

Is there more work to be done? Absolutely. But we should be proud of the progress made in the last several decades.

Condoleezza Rice, an African American woman from Alabama who served as US secretary of state, among other high offices, summed it up well:

The fact of the matter is we're not race-blind. Of course we still have racial tensions in the country. But the United States of America has made enormous progress in race relations, and it is the best place on earth to be a minority. . . . To my mind, the great thing about the United States of America is that you can be of any color, any ethnic group, any nationality, any religion and you can have dreams and aspirations that are your own, and then you can pursue them. That's what this country's about.[2]

Does our diversity make us a stronger or weaker nation?

It makes us stronger, no doubt about it. One of the things that makes this such a great country is that it's full of people with ancestries and backgrounds from all over the world. As the poet Walt Whitman wrote, "Here is not merely a nation but a teeming nation of nations."[3] That diversity gives us all a greater range of knowledge, experience, and perspective to draw on.

Our diversity is also an important sign of freedom. In this country, we are free to be different from one another. And because we are free, people from other places want to come here. They add even more to our diversity.

For each of us, our heritage is part of who we are. History and traditions matter—that's one of the beliefs central to conservatism. The best traditions of family and community need to be preserved.

The problem comes when we focus on our differences so much that we let them divide us. We begin to think of one another mainly in terms of ethnicity or class—as one of *them* instead of one of *us*.

The real danger comes when people use race, ethnicity, and other differences to turn groups against each other for political gain. That's politics of division, the kind that sends the message "That group over there wants to do your group harm." Black vs. white. Men vs. women. The rich vs. the rest. Diversity becomes not a reason for celebration but a cause of resentment. The politics of division make people think of themselves as victims who have been oppressed by others. It leads them to think the worst of people who are different.

E pluribus unum, one of the mottoes on every US coin, is an excellent guide. "Out of many, one." Our diversity comes from the *pluribus*—the many skin colors, backgrounds, and traditions we bring together. That's all to be celebrated.

The *unum* is the crowning part, though, the most important. In the end, we should think of ourselves as one people.

How are liberty and character connected in a free republic?

In his famous 1963 "I Have a Dream" speech in Washington, DC, the Rev. Martin Luther King Jr. said, "I have a dream that my four little children will one day live in a nation where they will not be judged by the color of their skin but by the content of their character." He said that his dream was "deeply rooted in the American dream."

Dr. King knew that qualities like honesty, loyalty, and courage are what really matter about a person. In the end, a person's character and actions—which come largely as a result of character—determine our regard for him or her. Rightly or wrongly, we may draw initial impressions based on how someone looks. But eventually we come to see the content of his or her character.

Liberty and character are connected in a free nation

like the United States. Because we are free to say what we want and determine our own actions, our decisions continually affect our character. If we choose to work hard, play by the rules, and treat others fairly, it strengthens our character. If we choose to slide by with little effort or mistreat others, that's something else. Liberty can add shine to our character or cast light on its weaknesses.

A free nation needs people of good character to thrive. The people themselves are supposed to run a republic like the United States. That takes virtues like the courage to defend liberty, the responsibility to stay informed, and the self-discipline to obey laws.

The American founders realized that civility is an important virtue in a free people. The word *civility* comes from the Latin roots *civitas*, meaning "city," and *civis*, meaning "citizen." Civility is behavior worthy of citizens living in a city or in common with others.

Civility means more than courtesy or politeness. It means showing a general goodwill for others. John Adams wrote to his son John Quincy Adams, "Treat all the World with Modesty, Decency, and Respect."[4] That's still excellent advice for dealing with our fellow citizens.

Part 4

NATIONAL DEFENSE

There are many good lessons to be learned from the United States military—lessons about virtues such as duty, honor, courage, and loyalty. One of the most important lessons is that it is always necessary to protect what is good and right, for your country and for yourself. If you don't stand firm and fight when necessary for what is good, sooner or later you will lose it, and you may have a very hard time getting it back.

DEFENDING *a* GREAT NATION

THE ANCIENT GREEK COLONY OF SYBARIS on Italy's southern coast was once a flourishing place. The Sybarites carried on a prosperous trade with cities around the Mediterranean and built an immense fortune. The wealthier they became, however, the more time they spent dreaming up new ways to entertain themselves.

One day a flute player came up with the idea of teaching horses to dance. The Sybarites had a fine cavalry, and before long the sound of a pipe set every warhorse prancing, much to the citizens' delight.

Nearby lay the town of Croton. The small Croton army was no match for the Sybarite cavalry—until a spy reported that he had seen the Sybarite horses dancing to a flute. The Crotoniates immediately attacked Sybaris with an army led by shepherds playing flutes. When the Sybarite cavalry galloped out to meet them, its horses began to waltz to the music. The Crotoniate army swept the field, and Sybaris fell.

The story, recorded by the ancient writer Athenaeus in the third century, may at first seem like just a quaint old legend, but Athenaeus wrote it down because it contains ageless wisdom. Even in the twenty-first century—*especially* in the twenty-first century—a nation that is in many ways the envy of the world has much to lose if it lets its defenses down.

Why is America so worth defending?

Sometimes you'll hear people say that the "American way of life" is worth defending. The words conjure images of the prosperity which many Americans enjoy and to which most of us aspire—a good paycheck, a solid roof over our heads, the chance to build some wealth with hard work.

There are billions of people around the world who would give just about anything for such prosperity, and there are some enemies who would take it from us if they could. It's certainly worth defending.

But there are things, some rights and ideals that America stands for, that are more important than prosperity. Liberty. Equality before the law. The fundamental dignity of every individual. The chance to live to one's fullest potential. Throughout history, people have yearned to live in a place guided by America's founding ideals.

When people from other countries become citizens of the United States, they take an oath of allegiance. That oath contains a pledge to help defend the country:

I hereby declare, on oath, that I absolutely and entirely renounce and abjure all allegiance and fidelity to any foreign prince, potentate, state, or sovereignty, of whom or which I have heretofore been a subject or citizen; that I will support and defend the Constitution and laws of the United States of America against all enemies, foreign and domestic; that I will bear true faith and allegiance to the same; that I will bear arms on behalf of the United States when required by the law; that I will perform noncombatant service in the Armed Forces of

the United States when required by the law;
that I will perform work of national importance
under civilian direction when required by
the law; and that I take this obligation freely,
without any mental reservation or purpose of
evasion; so help me God.[1]

Notice that new citizens pledge to support and defend
not a president or territory, but "the Constitution and
laws of the United States of America." That includes
the ideals enshrined in our laws. It's an obligation we all
share, native-born and naturalized citizens alike.

Why does America need such a big, powerful military?

The world is full of threats to American security, from
Islamic terrorist groups like al-Qaeda and ISIS (the
Islamic State of Iraq and Syria) to aggressive governments in nations like North Korea, Iran, and Russia.
The American founders understood that threats
would always exist. That's why, in the preamble of the
Constitution, they stated that one of the main reasons
for establishing a new government was to "provide for
the common defense."

Defense is arguably the first and chief responsibility of the federal government. No other institution is capable of protecting the country from foreign attack.

The best way to preserve both our safety and our freedom is to maintain a powerful military to answer threats wherever they may arise—a policy known as "peace through strength." This policy does not mean having a large army in order to conquer territory or start wars. It means that maintaining a powerful military discourages enemies from attacking us because we possess the might to overwhelm them.

The concept of peace through strength has been around for a long time. George Washington, in his first State of the Union message to Congress, said that "to be prepared for war is one of the most effectual means of preserving peace."[2]

In 1980, when Ronald Reagan accepted the Republican presidential nomination, he reminded us that a strong United States military helps the cause not only of peace but of freedom:

We are not a warlike people. Quite the opposite. We always seek to live in peace. We resort to force infrequently and with great reluctance—and only after we have determined that it is absolutely necessary. We are awed—and rightly so—by the forces of destruction at loose in the world in this nuclear era. But neither can we be naive or foolish. Four times in my lifetime America has gone to war, bleeding the lives of its young men into the sands of beachheads, the fields of Europe and the jungles and rice paddies of Asia. We know only too well that war comes not when the forces of freedom are strong, but when they are weak. It is then that tyrants are tempted.[3]

Has the US military done more good or harm over time?

Critics of the United States, including some in this country, sometimes claim that the US military has done much harm overseas. They insist that the United States is an "imperialist" or "colonialist" power, wreaking its evil will on the people of the third world.

The truth is that, on balance, the US military has been an enormous force for good in the world. During the Revolutionary War, Americans fought to establish the first nation created so people could be free. During the Civil War, the Union army fought to preserve government by the people and to end American slavery. During World War I, Americans fought in the trenches of Europe to stop a catastrophe that was engulfing much of the world.

Twice in the twentieth century the United States led the way in saving the world from tyranny—first from the Axis powers, then from Soviet totalitarianism. In this century, American soldiers have bled in Afghanistan and Iraq to combat terrorism and end brutal regimes that subjugated millions. Over the decades, the US military has launched countless humanitarian and relief efforts, from aiding victims of natural disasters to rescuing ships at sea.

America's record is not spotless. There have been times when the US military was used for injustice, such as the forced removal of Native Americans from ancestral lands. And tragedy has come with every war. For example, there have been US drone attacks against terrorists in Afghanistan that, despite the military's best efforts, have killed innocent civilians.

But it's important to remember that throughout history other superpowers have used armies to conquer territory and build empires by force. America, with its unrivaled military, has chosen a different course. The fact is the United States has liberated more people from tyranny than any other nation in history.

If you live in some desperate part of the world with a dictator's boot on your neck and you see a group of soldiers coming over the hill with a flag, you hope and pray it's the American flag. Because the American soldier is a soldier you can be absolutely confident is there to help you.

The United States is the greatest defender of freedom in the world. It's a record every American can be proud of.

DEFEATING ISLAMIC TERRORISM

IF YOU'VE RECENTLY GRADUATED from high school, or perhaps will graduate soon, you're too young to remember the events of September 11, 2001. You've probably heard about them and perhaps studied them in school. But you may not realize the horror of that day.

Go online and spend a little time watching news reports from that morning. Be warned that some of what you'll see and hear will be disturbing. Listen to the disbelief in reporters' voices as they realize that two jetliners have deliberately plowed into the twin towers of the World Trade Center in New York City. Watch the shock on people's faces as they see bodies begin to fall to the streets and the panic that erupts when those huge buildings collapse.

Watch the footage of smoke pouring out of a gaping hole in the side of the Pentagon, the military's head-quarters in Arlington, Virginia, after another plane dove into it. Listen to people tell about the last words from loved ones aboard United Flight 93, who called when they realized their plane had been hijacked for another suicide mission, one the passengers foiled at the cost of their own lives.

It's hard to watch the videos from that day, but it's important. It's important because it's reality—real evil at work, and some real heroism as well.

Is Islamic terrorism something you or I really need to concern ourselves with?

For the most part, terrorism seems very far away. The atrocities we hear about on the news—the suicide bomb-ings, beheadings, and destruction—mostly take place in distant countries, especially the Middle East. Occasionally terrorism reaches our shores, but relatively seldom, at least so far. It's easy to think it's not something we need to be too concerned about since it doesn't directly affect us too much.

But we should be very concerned, because terrorism is evil erupting in the world.

There is something about human nature that inclines us to look the other way when evil comes along. We often want to pretend it's not there, or that it's not so serious, or that it will go away on its own.

People have averted their eyes from evil time and again in history. One of the most famous examples is the rise of Nazi Germany in the twentieth century. Many people kept refusing to recognize Hitler for the monster he was and kept hoping he'd leave them alone, even after World War II had started. But of course he didn't leave them alone.

Perhaps people tend to ignore or downplay evil as long as they can because it's tough to confront it. Standing up to evil usually means taking some very uncomfortable, even dangerous actions.

Here is another fact about evil: if nothing is done about it, it tends to spread. And terrorism is an evil that is very intent on spreading. Islamic jihadists are determined to impose totalitarian rule on Muslim lands and extend Islamic dominion over the world.

Bloody dominion is what ISIS has in mind. "Today our swords are unsheathed towards you, government and citizens alike!" it has warned Americans. "And we will not stop until we quench our thirst for your blood."[1]

When evil like Islamic terrorism erupts in the world, all good people should be alarmed. If not confronted, it will reach us. It already has on September 11, 2001, and on other occasions since, although not again on that scale. The next time may be worse.

Why do Islamic terrorists attack us?

There has been much theorizing about the root causes of Islamic terrorism. Some suggest it springs up in cultures overwhelmed by poverty, ignorance, and despair. The problem with that theory is that many terrorists come from middle-class backgrounds or better. Those who mastermind or finance terrorist operations are often wealthy, privileged people, like Osama bin Laden.

Islamic terrorists claim that they act in response to the sins of the United States and other Western nations, such as publishing pornography and establishing military bases in Saudi Arabia. They make these claims as they enslave women and slaughter "infidels" who do not share their beliefs.

Some say that America's support of Israel is a main cause of terrorists' rage against us. True, Islamic radicals have nothing but hatred for Israel (the "Little Satan," as they call it). But there is no reason to think that if the United States abandoned Israel, a staunch democratic ally, terrorists would suddenly grow fond of the "Great Satan" (as they call America) and stop their war against the "decadent" West.

Islamic terrorists are driven by a manic determination to force their religion and law on others. This is, at bottom, the age-old struggle between tyranny and freedom. Islamic radicals hate the freedom represented by Western democracy and will do all they can to replace it with their rule.

Faisal Shahzad, a Pakistani-American who tried and failed to explode a bomb in Times Square in 2010, told us exactly what his aim was. He told a judge, "If I am given a thousand lives, I will sacrifice them all for the sake of Allah fighting this cause, defending our lands, making the word of Allah supreme over any religion or system. . . . [T]he defeat of U.S. is imminent and will happen in the near future, inshallah ["Allah willing"], which will only give rise to the much awaited Muslim caliphate, which is the only true world order."[2]

What is the best way for the United States to respond to Islamic terrorism?

Jihadists are at war with us, and they have vowed to keep it up. They post threats on Facebook and Twitter such as "We are in your state / we are in your cities / we are in your streets. You are our goals anywhere."[3] ISIS has promised that "we will raise the flag of Allah in the White House."[4]

The United States must fight back as hard as it can. There really is no other choice when facing a dangerous enemy that is determined to destroy us.

This is a time when moral clarity is much needed—a time when Americans need to distinguish clearly between right and wrong. Radical Islam is evil staring us in the face, threatening to wipe out all we hold to be good. When good people fail to recognize evil for what it is, when they fail to meet it head-on with strength, evil has a way of overcoming good.

This is an enemy that thrives on appeasement. "Dealing with the pampered and effeminate Americans will be easy," Osama bin Laden predicted before the attacks on September 11, 2001.[5] He was wrong about America's response to 9/11. But his statement betrays a basic characteristic of terrorists. Like all tyrants, they prey on uncertainty and weakness. They generally do not attack where and when they think they will lose.

This is a long struggle. The only way this nation will have the perseverance to continue the fight is for us to remember what we are fighting for.

The United States has provided more freedom to more people than any other nation in history; it has provided a greater degree of equality to more people than any other nation in history; it has created more prosperity, and spread it more widely, than any other nation in history; it has brought more justice to more people than any other in history. Our open, tolerant, prosperous, peaceable society is the marvel and envy of the ages.

We cannot take our rights and freedoms for granted, because Islamic radicals have sworn to bring jihad against them. If we do not defend ourselves strenuously and fight back against those who intend to destroy us, we ourselves will be destroyed.

Part 5

TRADITIONAL VALUES

This country was founded on principles such as

equality before the law and the right to worship

God as we wish. America is at its best when

it lives up to such values. What is true of our

country is true of each of us. We're at our best

when we live up to age-old values such as honesty,

compassion, perseverance, and faith. In the end,

finding success in life is a moral endeavor.

UPHOLDING TRADITIONAL VALUES

THE PASSING OF WISDOM and traditional values from one generation to the next lies at the heart of conservatism. Every generation has the responsibility of preserving our best values, along with the customs and institutions that help pass those values to the next generation.

Throughout your childhood, your parents and other adults around you—perhaps grandparents, teachers, ministers, and coaches—have worked to teach you good values. At some point in the not-too-distant future, that same obligation will fall on you—if not toward your own children, then toward young people around you.

It's a solemn obligation. Transmitting our civilization's best values to the young is crucial in helping them grow up to live honorable, fulfilling lives.

On the other hand, when one generation fails to pass along traditional values, things can go very wrong. It leaves people without a clear sense of what's important, of the difference between right and wrong. That can ruin lives and harm entire cultures.

What are "traditional values"?

First and most important, traditional values include good moral values—old-fashioned virtues like honesty, courage, compassion, and responsibility. The moral values you hold make all the difference in how good your life is. That truth of the human condition has never changed and will never change.

Conservatives believe there are enduring moral truths in the universe. That is, there are rules of right and wrong behavior that have come down to us through the centuries and apply to all. Moral rules such as it's wrong to steal. It's good to help others in need. Do unto others as you would have them do unto you.

In many ways, trying to live by these rules is the

central part of life. The striving to acquire virtues like self-discipline and perseverance is perhaps the greatest challenge we all face. Life is, in essence, a moral and civic endeavor.

You don't have to be religious to have good moral values, but for many people, faith is the most vital part of morality. God anchors their sense of right and wrong. They believe that God has established the moral order of the universe. Faith lifts each person outside the self and inspires a larger sense of purpose.

None of us are born knowing right from wrong or having good moral values. These things have to be learned. That's why each generation must pass good values on to the next generation.

Conservatives believe that education is largely about the formation of good character. Young people acquire virtues like kindness and loyalty largely by practicing them until they become habits. They learn morality through the examples, expectations, and rules set by adults around them.

The family is the most important institution when it comes to forming character. The moral lessons parents teach make all the difference. That's a big reason conservatives are so concerned about the breakdown of the American family and the fact that so many children are growing up in homes without both a mother and a father.

Conservatives want the traditional institution of marriage to thrive because it helps keep families together. Strong marriages are not only good for men and women, they're also the best way to raise children and give them solid values.

Community institutions play critical roles in teaching good moral values. Institutions like churches, synagogues, and other houses of worship. Schools. Neighborhoods. Volunteer groups such as the Boy Scouts and Girl Scouts and the Boys & Girls Clubs of America.

In fact, the entire culture is involved in transmitting values from one generation to the next. That includes the popular culture—the movies we watch, the books we read, the advertisements we see on TV, the music we download. Some of the messages our popular culture sends—like "do whatever makes you happy" and "it's fine to sleep around"—are directly opposed to traditional values. They're the kind of values that can get us in trouble.

How do traditional values help us in life?

Most of us don't give a lot of time to thinking about our character. We tend to focus on all sorts of other things—how much money we have, what sort of house we live in or job we have, how happy we feel.

But as the ancient Greek philosophers remind us, the unexamined life is not worth living. Our character is definitely worth our attention because, for one thing, it makes all the difference in how our lives turn out.

Character is made up largely of the values we hold and the way we put them into action. Cultivating "traditional values" may sound old fashioned and stuffy, especially when we're young. Yet those values turn out to be crucial both practically and morally.

Traditional values help make us more successful. Virtues like dedication and self-discipline still often mean the difference between achievement and failure. They help us financially in getting a promotion, building a company, or saving up a nest egg. They help us in *any* endeavor, from getting an A on a paper to making a strong marriage.

The poet Henry Wadsworth Longfellow wrote a

simple verse that reminds us of the link between success and virtues like perseverance and hard work:

> *The heights by great men reached and kept*
> *Were not attained by sudden flight,*
> *But they, while their companions slept,*
> *Were toiling upward in the night.*[1]

Traditional values help make us happier. True happiness isn't something we can chase and catch. It comes to us when we put time-tested virtues into action. For example, most of us learn that there is much more joy in a job well done than in shirking work. Dedication to a just cause. Generosity toward someone who needs help. Loyalty to a friend. These bring real contentment.

Traditional values help make us better people. To a large degree, they determine whether we live life well. They give us reliable standards of right and wrong. In its highest sense, life is a spiritual and moral journey. The values we carry with us help us choose which direction we take. They remind us of what is good and lasting. And they bring us closer to God.

MARRYING *and* RAISING *a* FAMILY

The traditional American family—one with a mother and father who are married and raising their children together—is in bad shape. Fewer Americans are getting married today than fifty years ago. Four out of ten babies in this country are born to unmarried women.[1] Many of them will grow up without ever knowing their fathers. As many as half of all American children will spend some time living with just one parent.[2]

It's very bad news for our country. The family is the fundamental building block of our civilization. As it falls apart, we see all sorts of bad effects: higher crime rates, poorer education, a less affluent society.

The good news is that for those who take it seriously, getting married and raising a family is still one of the most wonderful experiences of life. Even if marriage is far from your mind (and it most likely is at your age), it's worth thinking a little about what it means and why it's so important.

Why is the traditional American family breaking down?

There is no single cause of the breakdown of the traditional family. Shifts in people's values, habits, and attitudes have brought on changes.

One big cause is the modern emphasis on the self. Our culture is full of messages like "Do your own thing," "Make your own rules," and "Don't let others define you." They're very American messages, in a way—ones about individualism and personal freedom. The problem is that people use that kind of thinking to justify selfish behavior like fathering children and then walking away from them.

Many people view sex as a no-risk activity they can enjoy without marriage. *As long as we use contraceptives or the morning-after pill,* they tell themselves, *there's nothing to worry about. Why tie ourselves down?*

When they do get married, many view it not as a sacred obligation but as a contract, one that can always be broken. If they start to feel unhappy or bored, they just get out. Some marriages need to end, of course, especially in cases of spousal abuse. But far too many marriages end because people feel they have no moral duty to continue them, and because they can easily obtain a divorce.

Living in an affluent society like the United States can put pressure on marriage. The more we have, the more we want, sometimes at the expense of relationships. Husbands and wives often spend more time at work and less time with family. If not enough attention is paid, marital bonds can come undone.

Meanwhile, many poor young women who get pregnant don't want to marry the fathers of their children because they don't trust them. They believe the men don't work enough or earn enough money or are too violent.[3]

All these factors and more have harmed the traditional family. Unfortunately, there are few signs that things will get better anytime soon.

Why are traditional families so important?

The traditional family—a husband and wife living with their children—is vital to civilization's success. It is society's fundamental institution, the one where crucial lessons are taught.

Family is where the first and most important moral training takes place. Children aren't born knowing the difference between right and wrong. They have to learn how to be honest, brave, responsible, and kind. Teaching virtues is perhaps a parent's highest calling, and attention to virtues is one of the important ties that binds a family together.

Parents teach crucial lessons in several ways. They teach by example. When children witness parents working hard, treating others kindly, and taking responsibility for their own actions, they are apt to behave the same way.

Parents teach by setting high expectations, establishing rules, and talking about right and wrong. Countless daily lessons—getting homework done on time, choosing the right friends, speaking respectfully to others—shape the kind of adults young people eventually become.

There is much evidence to show that, generally

speaking, children who grow up without both a mother and a father in the home are more likely to struggle. For example, children raised by single parents are not as likely to do well in school or to get a college degree as children raised by married parents. They are more likely to engage in delinquent and illegal behavior. A child living with a single mother is four to five times as likely to be poor as a child raised by married parents.[4]

None of this means that a single mom or dad can't raise children well. Many do, and those children grow up to be fine, successful adults. But it does mean that it's much harder for one parent than it is for two. Single parents often find themselves spread too thin. Married parents can share responsibilities, so it's easier to spend time with children, set expectations, and enforce rules. The more two-parent families our country has, the better off it is.

Why should people get married in this day and age?

There's a good chance that sometime during the next several years, you'll fall in love and think about marriage. If you're like a lot of people these days, you may wonder if you really need it. After all, if you have each other, who needs a marriage certificate? It's your love that counts, right? Besides, do you really want that kind of obligation?

First of all, there are some good practical reasons to get married. Married people tend to enjoy better physical health and psychological well-being. They're usually better off financially than unmarried people. Married couples report greater sexual satisfaction. They're likely to live longer.[5]

More important, there are some powerful moral reasons to marry. Marriage is an obligation, but it is that obligation that makes marriage good—good for you, for your loved one, and for the children you may have.

"Wilt thou love her, comfort her, honor and keep her, in sickness and in health, in sorrow and in joy; and forsaking all others, keep thee only unto her so long as ye both shall live?"

Those words come from an old wedding ceremony, which many people still use today in one form or another. A man who lives up to that vow lifts himself morally. In devoting himself to his wife, he raises his own expectations of himself. In good marriages, men and women try to improve themselves for the sake of their spouse.

They also improve themselves for the sake of their

children. There is an old Aesop's fable about a mother crab and her child scurrying over the sand. The mother scolds her child, "Stop walking sideways! It's much more becoming to stroll straightforward." The young crab replies, "I will, Mother, just as soon as I see how. Show me the straight way, and I'll walk in it behind you."

The obligation of marriage demands that we try to improve ourselves for the sake of others. It demands that we put aside some of our own wants to care for others. It's a sacred obligation, and it can be one of the greatest blessings and joys of life.

RESPECTING LIFE

ABORTION IS THE FORCED ENDING OF A PREGNANCY resulting in the death of the embryo or fetus—in other words, the death of a developing baby. Most conservatives share a deep concern about abortion. This chapter explains why.

About a million abortions are performed in the United States every year. Thankfully, that number is down from a peak of 1.6 million in 1990. It is still a staggering, heartbreaking number. Well over fifty million abortions were performed in the four decades following *Roe v. Wade*, the 1973 Supreme Court ruling that made abortion legal throughout the country. That's about forty times the number of Americans lost in all of this nation's wars.[1]

Abortion is a highly personal issue. For some people, it causes sharp divides in political debate. It makes others so uncomfortable, they don't like to discuss it. As troubling as it may be, it's an issue that deserves careful thought.

Why do many Americans believe abortion is deeply wrong?

Because they believe that abortions kill helpless unborn babies and often cause great pain to their mothers. And because this is a moral issue that tells us what kind of society we are. Do we have a culture that values human life or one that regards it as disposable?

This nation was founded on the idea that every individual life has value. The Declaration of Independence says, "We hold these truths to be self-evident, that all men are created equal, that they are endowed by their Creator with certain unalienable rights, that among these are life, liberty and the pursuit of happiness." That idea set us apart from regions of the world where rulers treated life as something cheap and expendable.

If we still believe that every life has value, then protecting life is our moral duty. And, conservatives believe, it should be the legal duty of our government.

Some people believe there is a category of unborn children definitely not worth saving—babies who will be born with mental or physical disabilities. They believe those babies should be aborted for their own good and for the good of us all.

In 2014 Richard Dawkins, a famous evolutionary biologist, answered a woman who wrote on Twitter that she wouldn't know what to do if she were "pregnant with a kid with Down Syndrome." Dawkins tweeted, "Abort it and try again. It would be immoral to bring it into the world if you have the choice."[2]

Think about the cruelty of that statement for a minute. You may know or have met someone with Down syndrome. If so, you know that children with Down syndrome can live rewarding lives and bring much love, joy, and inspiration to others. Would you be willing to say, "You should never have been born" to such a person?

What other imperfections should disqualify someone from being born? A cleft palate? A missing limb? A heart defect? And who sets the standards about who lives and who dies?

What business does anyone have telling women what they can do with their own bodies?

Abortion rights supporters often say that abortion is a woman's choice and no one else's because it involves her body. The problem with this argument is that there is another life involved, the life of the unborn child. If we believe in the value of human life, then we have to take that child into account as well.

"What you are calling a 'child' is not a human life," pro-choice advocates might argue. "It's not a person yet, so it's all right to abort it."

Anyone who has seen a sonogram of a baby in the womb has to have questions about the "it's not a human life" argument. The pictures of tiny, growing fingers, toes, and faces make it hard to believe that we're looking at something other than a child.

Even without the evidence of sonograms, common sense and ethics tell us there's something wrong with the "it's not a human life" claim. When you were inside your mother's womb, you were less developed than you are now (just as an infant is less developed than a teenager), but you were you. There was nothing else in the womb that you swapped places with before birth. That was you. If you were not a human life, what in the world were you?

There is a reason mothers say, "I'm having a baby" when they're pregnant. They know they're carrying more than a "blob of tissue" inside. They're carrying exactly what they say: a baby.

Sometimes women face serious health concerns that require agonizing decisions about having an abortion. But the fact is that at least nine out of ten abortions in this country are elective procedures involving healthy women with healthy unborn babies. The most common reasons women give for having abortions are they're "not ready" for a child, or the "timing is wrong," or they "can't afford a baby now."[3]

The question is, are those good reasons for ending a life?

What does science have to say about the beginning of human life?

Thanks to advances in medical research, scientists know a lot about how a baby grows in the womb, and they're learning more every day. It's getting harder and harder for abortion supporters to say, "That's not a human life."

When a human sperm enters and joins a human ovum (egg), a living human embryo comes into being. From the very beginning, that embryo has a genetic composition that is distinctly human. When you were in your mother's womb, even at that early stage, your DNA contained the design that makes you unique—your blood type, your height, the color of your hair and eyes, the shape of your nose.

Human development proceeds at an amazingly fast rate. By about the sixth week of pregnancy, a baby's tiny heart has started to beat. By week seven, the baby's body is forming every organ it will need, including lungs, liver, kidneys, and intestines. Little arms and legs are starting to grow.

At eight weeks, a tiny face appears with the beginnings of two eyes, a nose, ears, and mouth. By week ten, connections are forming inside the brain. At twelve weeks, little teeth, fingers, and toes have formed.[4]

By twenty-two weeks of gestation, and possibly earlier, an unborn child can feel pain. This raises disturbing questions about what a baby experiences during an abortion.[5]

At twenty-three weeks, it's possible for a baby to survive outside the womb. More than 90 percent of babies born at twenty-seven to twenty-eight weeks in the United States survive a premature birth.[6]

We can always have political, philosophical, and religious debates about when life inside the womb becomes a person or "fully human." While we have those debates, we might want to ask ourselves, *Isn't erring on the safe side the right thing to do? If we're not exactly sure when human life begins, shouldn't we take care to protect what may be life?*

Meanwhile, the scientific evidence keeps building. It deserves serious, thoughtful consideration.

NOURISHING FAITH
in GOD

Oh! Almighty and Everlasting God, Creator of heaven, earth and the universe: Help me to be, to think, to act what is right, because it is right; make me truthful, honest and honorable in all things. Make me intellectually honest for the sake of right and honor and without thought of reward to me. Give me the ability to be charitable, forgiving and patient with my fellowmen— help me to understand their motives and their shortcomings—even as Thou understandest mine! Amen, Amen, Amen.

This was Harry S. Truman's favorite prayer. He said it as a high schooler, a drugstore clerk, a railroad time-keeper, a farmer, and as president of the United States during World War II and the Cold War.[1]

A firm belief in God runs through American history. The freedom to worship God as we please—or not to worship, if we choose—is part of our country's greatness. Each of us has the opportunity to become more honorable in all things, as Harry Truman's prayer says, by nourishing our faith.

Is it true that this country's founding principles are rooted in the Christian and Jewish religions?

Yes. America's founding principles are rooted in several sources, from the writings of ancient Greek and Roman philosophers to the essays of Enlightenment figures such as John Locke. The Jewish and Christian faiths— sometimes called the "Judeo-Christian tradition"—were a vital source of ideals.

Most of this country's founders were people of faith. They were overwhelmingly Christian, and in forging this nation, they looked to God. For example, when George Washington became president in 1789, one of his first official acts was to ask the blessing of "the Great Author of every public and private good."[2]

The Bible was the most widely available book in early America, and the founders naturally looked to it for guiding principles. When they opened their Bibles, they found this remarkable truth: God knows every individual's name, and he loves even the lowliest of his creatures. It was an idea that had taken root in the Jewish faith centuries earlier. The ancient Hebrew people had come to believe that each human being is important to God, that each matters equally in his eyes. In the days of Abraham and Isaac—a time of cultures that believed in many ruthless gods who killed men for sport—that was a radical thought.

Later religions, including Christianity, took up and spread this idea that all are equal in God's sight. In 1776 that deeply spiritual belief became the basis for the American ideal, spelled out in the Declaration of Independence, that "all men are created equal."

The founders believed that all men are born with certain rights that are not subject to the whims of kings, such as the right to life and the right to control one's own property. These rights, the founders believed, came not from the minds of men or from governments but from God. As the Declaration famously put it, all men "are endowed by their Creator with certain unalienable rights."

Why is freedom of religion crucial in America?

One of the "unalienable rights" named in the Declaration is the right to liberty. The founders believed that God creates all people to be free. He endows them with free will—the freedom to choose between right and wrong, to live a good life, to live to their fullest potential. Freedom, then, is a sacred gift. The founders were determined to set up a government that would not take it away from people, as so many kings and tyrants had done.

The founders realized that if American democracy was to work, it would need religion as an ally. A government elected by the people relies on the people to make good decisions. Making good decisions takes wisdom and virtue. Therefore, a successful democracy requires a citizenry of sound moral character. The founders believed that religion provides the best anchor for such national character.

This is not to say the founders believed that only religious individuals could possess good character.

But they knew that religion helps people be good, and they were convinced that their experiment in self-government would fail without a religious population. As John Adams wrote, "Our Constitution was made only for a moral and religious people. It is wholly inadequate to the government of any other."[3]

The founders made freedom of religion a fundamental principle for the new country. The First Amendment in the Bill of Rights says that "Congress shall make no law respecting an establishment of religion, or prohibiting the free exercise thereof." The founders decided not to establish a national church or to favor any particular religion, as England and other nations had done. In their view, that was the best way to keep religion and civil government from interfering with each other.

They wanted Americans to be a religious people, but they realized that a government that tried to force religion on citizens was asking for trouble. Faith is a matter of the heart and soul, and if worship is not given freely, it is not true faith. Liberty is the ground on which faith can grow.

For all of these reasons, religious liberty is a pillar of American freedom. It is the foundation of the American ideals of human equality, human dignity, and freedom of conscience. Take it away—take away a person's right to seek spiritual truth—and all other freedoms are at risk.

How does faith help us?

When they graduate from school, many young people enter a stage of life when they give little thought and time to their faith. Life gets busy, and there are, after all, so many other things to do.

Here is one of the best pieces of advice anyone can give you as you make your way into the world: nourish your faith. Find a community of fellow believers. Make time to worship communally. Perhaps join a group that studies Scripture. Feed your soul.

Nourishing your faith brings you closer to God, and that in itself is reason enough to make the effort. There are also some good, practical benefits.

Nourishing your faith will improve your character. It will help you gain virtues like kindness, patience, generosity, courage, and self-control.

It will improve your mind. Religious thought involves humanity's most profound questions and ideas. Reading or listening to Scripture exposes you to some of the most beautiful language ever written. You'll be smarter for it.

Nourishing your faith gives you direction in life's journey. It's easy to feel overwhelmed by the questions we face on that journey. *What am I supposed to do with myself? What will make me truly happy? What does it all mean?* Uncertainty can make all of us feel adrift at times. Faith helps us stop drifting by giving us some anchors and by reminding us of the things that really matter. It helps us set a course when we're ready to move ahead.

Nourishing your faith brings fellowship. It can help you find lifelong friends and loved ones. Once a man who was sitting with a minister beside a fireplace insisted that he didn't need church. The minister took some tongs, lifted a glowing coal from the fire, and set it apart. Before long the lone coal stopped glowing and turned black. The minister picked it up and placed it back against the other embers, and pretty soon it was glowing again. "We are much more alive when we live in fellowship with others," the minister said quietly, and he was right.

Finally, nourishing your faith helps you help others. It reminds you to shift your attention away from yourself. It inspires and equips you to serve those on the journey with you, and that makes the world a better place.

NOTES

A WORD OF ADVICE TO YOUNG AMERICANS

1. James Madison, *Federalist Papers*, no. 55, February 13, 1788.

Part 1: Free Enterprise

WORKING, STRIVING, ACHIEVING

1. Peter Wehner and Arthur C. Brooks, *Wealth and Justice: The Morality of Democratic Capitalism* (Washington, DC: AEI Press, 2011), 12–14.
2. Charles Dickens, *Hard Times*, chapter V.
3. Calvin Coolidge, "Speech on the Occasion of the One Hundred and Fiftieth Anniversary of the Declaration of Independence" (Philadelphia, July 5, 1926).

MAKING THE MOST OF OPPORTUNITIES

1. Michael Burlingame, *Abraham Lincoln: A Life*, vol. 1 (Baltimore: Johns Hopkins University Press, 2008), 567.
2. William J. Bennett, *The Book of Virtues* (New York: Simon & Schuster, 1993), 413.
3. Ron Haskins, "Getting Ahead in America," *National Affairs*, no. 1 (Fall 2009): 48, http://www.nationalaffairs.com/publications /detail/getting-ahead-in-america.

BEING A GOOD STEWARD

1. Matthew 25:14-30.
2. Matthew 19:24; Mark 10:25; Luke 18:25.

3. 2 Corinthians 9:7, KJV.
4. "Energy Overview," The World Bank, http://www.worldbank.org /en/topic/energy/overview#1.
5. US Environmental Protection Agency, Office of Mobile Resources, "Automobile Emissions: An Overview," Fact Sheet OMS-5 (August 1994), 4, http://www.epa.gov/otaq/consumer/05-autos.pdf.
6. Genesis 2:15.

Part 2: Limited Government

TAKING CHARGE OF OUR LIVES AND OUR GOVERNMENT

1. Bernard Bailyn, *The Ideological Origins of the American Revolution* (Cambridge, MA: Harvard University Press, 1992), 60.
2. Thomas Jefferson, letter to Edward Carrington, May 27, 1788.
3. Romina Boccia, "Federal Spending by the Numbers, 2014: Government Spending Trends in Graphics, Tables, and Key Points (Including 51 Examples of Government Waste)," The Heritage Foundation, December 8, 2014, http://www.heritage.org/research /reports/2014/12/federal-spending-by-the-numbers-2014.
4. Debt estimate figures from US Debt Clock.org, accessed November 2, 2015, http://www.usdebtclock.org/.
5. Merrill Matthews, "Government Programs Have Become One Big Scammer Fraud Fest," Forbes, January 13, 2014, http://www.forbes .com/sites/merrillmatthews/2014/01/13/government-programs-have -become-one-big-scammer-fraud-fest/.
6. Michael Puma et al., "Third Grade Follow-up to the Head Start Impact Study Final Report," OPRE Report #2012-45 (Washington, DC: Office of Planning, Research and Evaluation, Administration for Children and Families, U.S. Department of Health and Human Services, October 2012), http://www.acf.hhs.gov/programs/opre /resource/third-grade-follow-up-to-the-head-start-impact-study -final-report.

BEING SELF-RELIANT

1. Robert Rector, "Self-Sufficiency Rate Stagnates, Welfare State Grows," in *2014 Index of Culture and Opportunity*, ed. Jennifer A. Marshall

and Rea S. Hederman Jr. (The Heritage Foundation, 2014), 47–48, http://index.heritage.org/culture/.

2. Lawrence M. Mead, *From Prophecy to Charity: How to Help the Poor* (Washington, DC: AEI Press, 2011), 31.

3. Franklin D. Roosevelt, "Annual Message to Congress" (speech, Washington, DC, January 4, 1935).

4. Ralph Waldo Emerson, "Aristocracy," *The Works of Ralph Waldo Emerson.*

HANDLING OUR NATION'S FINANCES WISELY

1. Debt estimate figures from US Debt Clock.org, accessed November 2, 2015, http://www.usdebtclock.org/.

2. Romina Boccia, "Federal Spending by the Numbers, 2014: Government Spending Trends in Graphics, Tables, and Key Points (Including 51 Examples of Government Waste)," The Heritage Foundation, December 8, 2014, http://www.heritage.org/research /reports/2014/12/federal-spending-by-the-numbers-2014.

3. Compañía General de Tabacos de Filipinas v. Collector of Internal Revenue, 275 U.S. 87, 100 (1927), http://caselaw.lp.findlaw.com /cgi-bin/getcase.pl?court=us&vol=275&invol=87.

4. Kyle Pomerleau, "Tax Freedom Day 2015 Is April 24th," Tax Foundation, March 30, 2015, http://taxfoundation.org/article /tax-freedom-day-2015-april-24th.

5. Boccia, "Federal Spending by the Numbers, 2014."

6. Kyle Pomerleau and Andrew Lundeen, "Summary of Latest Federal Income Tax Data," Tax Foundation, December 22, 2014, http://taxfoundation.org/article/summary-latest-federal-income -tax-data-0.

7. See Luke 12:48.

Part 3: Individual Liberty

LIVING UP TO OUR RESPONSIBILITIES

1. William J. Bennett, *The Book of Virtues* (New York: Simon & Schuster, 1993), 217.

2. Abraham Lincoln, "Address before the Young Men's Lyceum of Springfield, Illinois" (speech, January 27, 1838).

KEEPING A SOUND MIND AND BODY

1. William J. Bennett and Robert A. White, *Going to Pot* (New York: Center Street, 2015), xiv.
2. Ibid., 6, 15–16, 20–21.
3. Ibid., 12–13, 28.
4. Ibid., 26, 139.
5. Ibid., 27.
6. Ibid., 25, 147.
7. Ibid., 153–54.
8. Ibid., 54.
9. William J. Bennett, *The De-valuing of America* (New York: Summit Books, 1992), 120.

Part 4: National Defense

TREATING OTHERS AS WE WOULD HAVE THEM TREAT US

1. See Luke 10:25-37.
2. Condoleezza Rice, interview on *Fox and Friends*, Fox News, November 6, 2014, http://video.foxnews.com/v/3878300052001 /condoleeza-rices-take-on-americas-political-landscape/.
3. Walt Whitman, preface to *Leaves of Grass*.
4. John Adams, letter to John Quincy Adams, May 14, 1783.

DEFENDING A GREAT NATION

1. "Naturalization Oath of Allegiance to the United States of America," Department of Homeland Security, June 25, 2014, http://www.uscis .gov/us-citizenship/naturalization-test/naturalization-oath-allegiance -united-states-america.
2. George Washington, "First Annual Message to Congress on the State of the Union" (speech, New York, January 8, 1790).
3. Ronald Reagan, "Address Accepting the Presidential Nomination at the Republican National Convention in Detroit" (speech, July 17, 1980).

DEFEATING ISLAMIC TERRORISM

1. "Full Text of the Last E-mail the Islamic State Sent to the Foley Family," *GlobalPost*, August 21, 2014, http://www.globalpost.com

/dispatch/news/regions/middle-east/syria/140821/text-last-email
-islamic-state-sent-foley-family.

2. William J. Bennett and Seth Leibsohn, *The Fight of Our Lives*
(Nashville: Thomas Nelson, 2011), xii.

3. Mark Suppelsa, "Photo Implies ISIS Threat to Chicago," WGNtv.com,
August 21, 2014, http://wgntv.com/2014/08/21/photo-implies-isis
-threat-to-chicago/.

4. Jamie Weinstein, "ISIS Threatens America: 'We Will Raise the Flag
of Allah in the White House,'" *Daily Caller*, August 8, 2014,
http://dailycaller.com/2014/08/08/isis-threatens-america-we-will
-raise-the-flag-of-allah-in-the-white-house/.

5. Bernard Lewis, *Faith and Power* (New York: Oxford University Press,
2010), 166.

Part 5: Traditional Values

UPHOLDING TRADITIONAL VALUES

1. Henry Wadsworth Longfellow, "The Ladder of St. Augustine."

MARRYING AND RAISING A FAMILY

1. Joyce A. Martin et al., "Births: Final Data for 2012," *National Vital
Statistics Reports*, vol. 62, no. 9, National Center for Health Statistics,
December 30, 2013, p. 7, Table C, http://www.cdc.gov/nchs/fastats
/unmarried-childbearing.htm.

2. Ron Haskins, "Marriage, Parenthood, and Public Policy," *National
Affairs*, no. 19 (Spring 2014), http://www.nationalaffairs.com
/publications/detail/marriage-parenthood-and-public-policy.

3. Ibid.

4. Ibid.

5. "The Benefits of Marriage," FamilyFacts.org, http://www.familyfacts
.org/briefs/1/the-benefits-of-marriage.

RESPECTING LIFE

1. "Abortion Statistics: United States Data and Trends," National
Right to Life Committee, February 2014, http://www.nrlc.org
/communications/abortionnumbers/.

2. Peter Wehner, "The Nasty, Brutish World of Richard Dawkins," *Commentary*, August 21, 2014, http://www.commentarymagazine .com/2014/08/21/the-nasty-brutish-world-of-richard-dawkins/.

3. Cathy Cleaver Ruse and Rob Schwarzwalder, "The Best Pro-Life Arguments for Secular Audiences," Family Research Council, http://www.frc.org/brochure/the-best-pro-life-arguments-for -secular-audiences.

4. "Your Growing Belly and Baby: A Timeline through Pregnancy," WebMD, http://www.webmd.com/baby/interactive-pregnancy-tool -fetal-development.

5. Arina Grossu, "What Science Reveals about Fetal Pain," Family Research Council, January 2015, http://frc.org/fetalpain.

6. "Newborn Loss: Neonatal Death," March of Dimes Foundation, January 2010, http://www.marchofdimes.org/loss/neonatal-death.aspx.

NOURISHING FAITH IN GOD

1. "Harry Truman's Favorite Prayer," Harry S. Truman Library and Museum, http://www.trumanlibrary.org/kids/prayer.htm.

2. William J. Bennett, *Our Sacred Honor: Words of Advice from the Founders in Stories, Letters, Poems, and Speeches* (New York: Simon & Schuster, 1997), 381.

3. Ibid., 370.

ABOUT THE AUTHORS

William J. Bennett is the former US Secretary of Education and current host of the seventh-ranked nationally syndicated radio program *Morning in America*. Bill is one of the nation's most respected voices on cultural, political, and educational issues. Bennett is the author of 24 books, including #1 *New York Times* bestsellers *The Book of Virtues* and *The Death of Outrage*.

John T. E. Cribb is an author whose previous work includes *The American Patriot's Almanac* (coauthored with Bill Bennett) and *The Educated Child* (coauthored with Bill Bennett and Chester Finn). He has collaborated with Bill Bennett on several books, including *The Book of Virtues*.

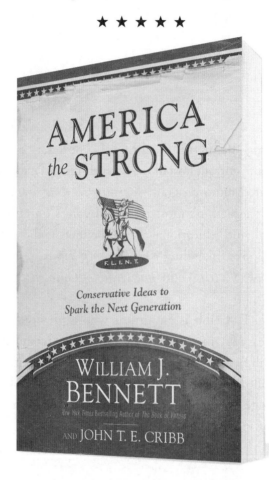